P9-DCV-029

WHO ARE
COMMUNITY
LEADERS?

by Martha E. H. Rustad

PEBBLE
a capstone imprint

Pebble Emerge is published by Pebble, an imprint of Capstone.
1710 Roe Crest Drive, North Mankato, Minnesota 56003
www.capstonepub.com

Library of Congress Cataloging-in-Publication data is available on the Library of Congress website.
ISBN 978-1-9771-2268-1 (library binding)
ISBN 978-1-9771-2612-2 (paperback)
ISBN 978-1-9771-2295-7 (eBook PDF)

Summary: All communities need leaders of some kind to help steer and shape them. Through their elected positions, jobs, or volunteer work, leaders are vital to a strong community. A question-and-answer format and photos with which kids can identify define leaders' responsibilities and how leaders cooperate with all citizens to achieve shared goals. A hands-on activity encourages active community participation.

Image Credits
Getty Images: Caiaimage/Martin Barraud, 7, Hero Images, 1; iStockphoto: kzenon, 20, SDI Productions, 5, 9, XiXinXing, 18; Shutterstock: Arisya, 17, ESB Professional, 19, justaa, (icon) cover, KelseyJ, 8, Monkey Business Images, 11, 15, Pressmaster, 13, Rawpixel.com, 6, 14, Sergey Novikov, 4, Victoria Kalinina, design element, wavebreakmedia, Cover, 12

Editorial Credits
Editor: Jill Kalz; Designer: Juliette Peters; Media Researcher: Morgan Walters; Production Specialist: Kathy McColley

Printed and bound in China.
3322

Table of Contents

Words in **bold** are in the glossary.

What Is a Leader?

Leaders go first. They show others what to do or not to do. They help others think smarter. Your parents can be leaders. You can be a leader. Anyone can!

Some leaders are in charge of big groups of people. Others lead small groups. A **community** leader helps people who live, work, and play together.

Leaders think about the needs of the whole community. They choose what is best for the group. Good communities are strong communities.

Community leaders also think about
each person. They treat everyone fairly.
They want everyone to be safe. That way,
the community can learn and grow.

Who Leads a Community?

A community has many leaders. The **mayor** is a leader. A community **elects** one person to be mayor. That person speaks for everyone in the community.

The **city council** also leads. This group of people is elected by the community. The city council studies problems and tries to fix them. It works with the mayor.

What Kinds of Leaders Are There?

Not all community leaders are elected. Some people lead in their daily jobs. Police officers and firefighters lead by keeping us safe. They also help people who are hurt. Doctors and **nurses** lead by keeping our bodies healthy.

Other community leaders help us learn. Teachers help us read and think. Librarians use books and computers to answer our questions. Coaches teach us teamwork.

Farmers are leaders too. We need healthy food to stay strong. Farmers give us that food. They grow fruit and vegetables. They raise animals.

Who Can Be a Leader?

Are you a good listener? Do you work well with others? If you see a problem, can you find a way to **solve** it? If so, you can be a leader!

Good leaders have plans and goals.
They **convince** others to help them.
Good leaders speak up. They make sure
that no one is left out.

Mario listens to his friends. They talk about the dirty park nearby. Mario sees a problem to solve. He gathers people to pick up garbage in the park.

Mario thinks. How can he keep the park clean? He asks the city council for more garbage bins. Now everyone can enjoy the park safely. Mario is a leader.

PLEASE USE ME

17

Clara sees a problem. The town library needs books. How can she help? Clara has no money to spend. She asks people to give books as gifts to the library. They do!

Now the library has books. It shares them with everyone. Clara saw a problem and solved it. She asked others for help. Clara is a leader. How can you be a leader?

19

Get Involved: Be a Community Leader

Anyone can be a community leader. Watch and listen. Be kind. Find a way to lead. Be sure to ask an adult for help.

What You Need:

- a willingness to do good things

What You Do:

1. Think about places in need of help in your community. Is there an animal shelter nearby? How about a community garden or a nursing home?

2. Ask if you can help. Offer to walk shelter dogs or cuddle with shelter cats. Donate pet food, leashes, or blankets. Water plants or pull weeds in the garden. Play games or sing songs with people in the nursing home.

3. Be a leader. Ask others to help you. Find a way to give back to your community.

Glossary

city council (SI-tee KOWN-suhl)—a group of people chosen to lead a community

community (kuh-MYOO-nuh-tee)—a group of people who live, work, and play together

convince (kuhn-VINSS)—to talk someone into following a certain path

elect (i-LEKT)—to choose someone as a leader by voting

mayor (MAY-ur)—the leader of a city

nurse (NURSS)—a person trained to take care of sick people, usually in a hospital

solve (SOLV)—to find the answer to a problem

Read More

Lindeen, Mary. *Very Important People.* Chicago: Norwood House Press, 2020.

Mason, Paul. *25 Fun Things to Do for Your Neighbors.* Minneapolis: Hungry Tomato, 2019.

Internet Sites

Serve in Your Community
https://www.nationalservice.gov/serve

35+ Service Projects for Kids
https://kidworldcitizen.org/35-service-projects-for-kids

Index

AMERICA IS UNDER ATTACK

AMERICA IS UNDER ATTACK

BY DON BROWN

Rb
Flash
Point

ROARING BROOK PRESS
New York

A bright morning sun lit a cloudless blue sky.

America started its day. Highways filled with traffic. Railroads rumbled with trains. Airports roared with jetliners.

Among the hundreds of planes rising into that flawless blue sky were two from Boston, one from Newark, New Jersey, and one from Washington, D.C. Among their ordinary passengers were nineteen deadly men.

They were followers of Osama Bin Laden, leader of an organization known as al-Qaeda. The group hated America's power and influence. Bin Laden promised violence against America. The nineteen men had pledged their lives to fulfill that threat.

At 8:00 AM on September 11, 2001, they acted.

With knives, pepper spray, and threats of bombs, they stormed the four airliner cockpits and wrested control away from the pilots. The jets were no longer just ordinary airplanes; they were weapons. The planes banked away from their planned flight paths and headed for their targets.

On one of the planes, a flight attendant managed to alert on-the-ground authorities to the hijacking. She reported, "Something is wrong . . . We are flying very, very low."

Before them loomed the World Trade Center on the lower tip of New York's Manhattan Island. Each skyscraping tower was just over 1,350 feet tall and boasted 110 floors. More than 14,000 early-bird workers had already arrived, a fraction of the 50,000 who worked there.

At 8:46 AM, the plane slammed into the North Tower.

Flying at 450 miles per hour, the jet exploded through floors 93 to 99. The earth shook. Debris and flames hurtled from the opposite side of the building.

Fire Chief Joseph Pfiefer was out with a truck and his crew in lower Manhattan when he heard the plane approach. He looked up and watched the jet smash into the tower.

"Everyone . . . get in the rigs because we're going down there," he said.

Inside the tower, an inferno of jet fuel shot down a thousand feet of elevator shaft to the lobby and lower levels.

"I heard a roar," said police captain Anthony Whitaker, who had been standing his regular, early morning watch at the base of the tower. "I saw a gigantic fireball . . . I turned . . . and ran."

The building suffered horrible damage. People on lower floors could escape down the stairs. But hundreds of others on higher floors were trapped by burning wreckage and ruined stairwells. Many used their cell phones to call for help—three thousand calls were made to the 911 emergency system in the ten minutes after the crash. Overloaded circuits made connections difficult. Trapped people were told to wait for help.

Chief Pfiefer and his team marched into the North Tower and sent out the alarm for more firefighters. They and other rescue workers quickly arrived, sirens blaring. Emergency vehicles flooded lower Manhattan. Within seventeen minutes of the crash, a thousand fire, police, and rescue workers swarmed the World Trade Center. Many were off duty; they simply reported to the scene when they heard the news.

Among the rescue workers arriving at the North Tower was Chief Pfiefer's brother Kevin, a lieutenant in the fire department. The two men shared a few moments together, then turned to their duties. The chief remained in the lobby to direct the arriving firefighters. His brother headed for the crash site.

Two companies of firefighters were ordered up to the flaming wreckage ninety stories above. They entered a stairwell and began the thousand foot vertical climb. Each fire fighter carried more than 80 pounds of equipment. Without elevators, it would take more than an hour to reach the impact site.

"We started up . . . from the ground floor. We would take it ten floors at time [and] catch our breath," said a fire captain. "This way, we would have some energy to . . . do whatever we were going to do when we got to the upper floors."

The fire department's plan wasn't to fight the fire.

"Fire [fighting] systems in the building were probably damaged and possibly inoperable . . . So we determined early on, that this was going to be strictly a rescue mission. We were . . . going to get people out, and then we were going to get out," said a fire chief.

The fire department ordered everyone out of the building.

A total tower evacuation had never been attempted before. It had never been practiced, nor even been planned. No one had imagined a catastrophe that would require it.

Meanwhile, Captain Whitaker—the police captain who'd earlier dodged the fireball in the tower lobby—ordered a full evacuation of the World Trade Center, the collection of buildings that was home to the Twin Towers.

Poor communications and a damaged public address system made it nearly impossible to broadcast the evacuation order. People in the buildings continued to receive mixed messages from emergency operators; sometimes to "stay put" and other times to "leave immediately." Some people left, others departed and returned.

In the North Tower, the fire department even had trouble contacting their fire fighters as they climbed the stairs to the impact zone. Their handheld radios barely operated. Making and receiving orders was hit or miss.

High on the 88th floor, Frank De Martini, the building's construction manager, hadn't heard anything from the rescue operation based in the lobby. He didn't even know about the plane crash; he thought someone had planted a bomb or that a mechanical room had exploded. His office was wrecked. The ceiling had collapsed, flames licked the walls, and smoke filled the air. Dazed people stumbled about. He surveyed the ruins, gathered a team, and went to work.

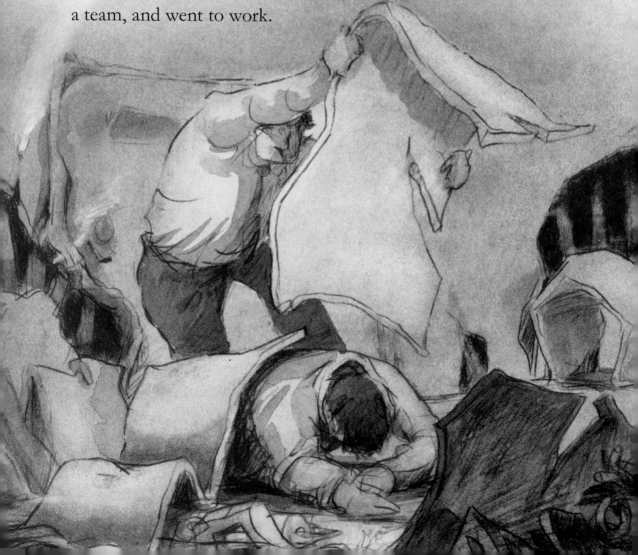

First, De Martini discovered an open stairway and sent down more than twenty-five people who had been trapped. Among them was his eighty-nine-year-old co-worker Moe Lipson.

"My heart was pumping harder than usual," Moe said.

Then De Martini, along with co-worker Pablo Ortiz and others, made their way up to the 89th floor. They found more people trapped by debris and freed them, sending the rescued people down the stairwell. De Martini and Ortiz continued up toward an unknowable chaos, looking for more trapped survivors.

The floors at the crash site were a tangle of burning wreckage. Smoke billowed across lower Manhattan. On the floors above the burning rubble, hundreds of people were trapped. Using phones and email, in voices sometimes calm and other times frantic, they sent the same message: We're stuck! Send help!

Police helicopters flew close.

"People were hanging out of the building, gasping for air," said a helicopter crew member. "There was no way of getting near anyone in a window . . . we were helpless, totally helpless."

Heavy smoke and intense heat from the fire made rescuing people from the roof impossible.

Some of the trapped people jumped.

Suddenly a helicopter pilot shouted, "There's a second plane!"

Stanley Praimnath saw the second jet race straight at his 81st floor office in the South Tower. He dived under his desk, screaming.

Everything exploded. Walls and ceilings collapsed. Part of the jet's wing jammed into a door. The overpowering stink of jet fuel made breathing difficult.

But Praimnath was alive; the only survivor at the heart of the impact.

The second hijacked jetliner had crashed through the 77th to 85th floors of the South Tower. Massive flames spewed from the tower. Wreckage rained down on the street.

It was 9:03 AM, seventeen minutes after the strike on the North Tower.

People now understood the earlier crash was not a freak accident but a deliberate attack.

Despite the horrific crash, one stairwell in the South Tower remained intact. Unlike the North Tower, people above the crash had the means to escape to the street. In the chaos, however, many people would not find it.

Firefighters scrambling into the South Tower discovered a working elevator that carried them to the 40th floor. From there, they climbed a stairwell. Passing them on the way down were escaping civilians. The lack of panic by the civilians impressed the firefighters. People patted the fire fighters' backs and wished them well. In return, the firefighters encouraged them for their long flight down.

Below, one elevator screeched to a halt at the building's main lobby. It had plunged 900 feet before automatic safety brakes stopped it. The riders pried open the doors and escaped.

In the North Tower, another elevator sat stalled and locked closed at the lobby. It had come to a halt when the plane struck. Chris Young, its lone occupant, knew nothing of the catastrophe around him. Firefighters going up couldn't hear his shouts and marched past him, unaware of his predicament.

High above was another trapped elevator. From its intercom, the riders learned there had been an "explosion." The riders forced open the doors and discovered they had stopped in front of a wall. One of the passengers was a window washer. He began scratching the wall with the metal edge of his squeegee to make a hole.

Dense smoke billowed off both towers. Falling wreckage hurtled to the ground. Despite the risk, hundreds of firefighters, police, emergency medical technicians, private security guards, and even workers from the neighboring hotel stationed themselves around the World Trade Center, tending to the injured and helping office workers flee. To avoid the debris raining down on the plaza outside the tower, they directed evacuees through neighboring buildings or through underground corridors. Thousands streamed away.

At 9:37 AM 200 miles away from the disaster zone in New York, the military's headquarters in Washington, D.C., known as the Pentagon became the third target of the hijackers' attack. The jet swooped low and plowed into the building at ground level. The flaming impact nearly reached the center courtyard.

"It was a loud roar . . . The building shook . . . Jet fuel poured into the corridors . . . and ignited, taking all the oxygen out of the air," said an Army officer.

"The heat inside was so hot, it felt like the sun kissing you," said a soldier.

Rescuers raced to the scene. From exits everywhere, 20,000 people eventually evacuated the building.

Back in New York, in the wreckage of the South Tower, Stanley Praimnath yelled, "Help! Help! I'm buried! Is anybody there?"

Brian Clark was there.

He had been fleeing his ruined office when he'd heard shouts. Clark and Praimnath clawed the rubble. Clark yanked the trapped man free, and the two fell to the floor in a hug.

"I'm Brian," Clark said.

"I'm Stanley," Praimnath said.

The two men found a stairwell and headed down.

Thousands of people escaped down the towers' stairwells. The injured, the old, the handicapped were helped by friends, by strangers. People shared drinks. A blind man came down with his guide dog. Two brothers trudged the stairwells: one, a firefighter, going up, the other, a businessman, coming down. They didn't meet.

Not on the stairs were co-workers Ed Beyea and Abe Zelmanowitz. Beyea was paralyzed and in a wheelchair. There wasn't an elevator for him to escape. Zelmanowitz waited with his friend for rescue. There were eventually joined by Fire Captain William Burke. Together the three waited for available rescue workers to carry Beyea down.

By 10:00 AM, lines of firefighters stretched all the way to the 54th floor in the North Tower. At the same time in the South Tower, one hard charging chief made it all the way to the impact zone on the 78th floor. Chief Orio Palmer used the elevator to travel forty stories and then raced up thirty-eight flights of stairs on foot.

Hundreds of miles away, another kind of desperate action unfolded. The fourth hijacked plane was still in the air, creasing the Pennsylvania sky. By way of cell phone calls to the ground, passengers learned of the attacks in New York and Washington. The passengers decided they had to fight back.

They stormed the cockpit. The hijacker pilot pitched and banked the plane to throw the passengers off balance. At 10:03 AM, the jet rolled onto its back and roared earthward. The passengers were still battling when the plane smashed into a field in Shanksville, Pennsylvania.

Meanwhile in New York, molten aluminum poured from the South Tower as the remains of the jetliner melted.

Watching the disaster was a city building engineer, one of the many government officials who had rushed to the scene. Surveying the damage he warned fire department commanders that the tower was close to collapsing. The warning came too late: at 9:59 AM the South Tower came down. In ten seconds, the mammoth building was reduced to rubble.

"It looked exactly like an avalanche coming down the street at you," a policeman said.

It cleaved a neighboring hotel in two.

Cars flew through the air. Giant steel girders tumbled like toothpicks.

"We saw air conditioning ducts. We saw parts of buildings. And newspapers and debris, all in a dust ball coming at us!" said a police captain.

The collapse generated a furious wind.

One police officer was thrown from one side of the street to the other. "I was literally blown out of my shoes," she said.

A monstrous, dirty cloud covered everything.

"Picture taking . . . flour and sticking it up your nose and in your mouth. That's what breathing was like," said another officer. "At the same time, I'm feeling debris hitting . . . my legs, hitting my ankles, hearing it pile up above me."

Fire Chief Pfiefer and the other firefighters in the North Tower lobby heard a rumble.

"I thought . . . something was crashing through the lobby . . . We . . . huddled down at the base of the escalator. [The] whole area . . . became totally black," Pfiefer said. "We stayed there until the rumbling stopped. I never even suspected that the second tower collapsed."

In the North Tower lobby, the doors of a stalled elevator opened. The collapse of the South Tower had cut the power to the elevator's door locks. From the car emerged Chris Young, the trapped passenger who'd been overlooked by rescue workers. Earlier he had boarded the elevator from a polished, modern lobby. Now he shuffled through clouds of dust, over rubble and debris.

Alone.

Pfiefer and the other firefighters had fled the lobby when the wreckage of the South Tower billowed through.

Up to that moment, few people believed the buildings could be brought down. They had been designed to survive a jetliner collision. The towers had survived a massive terrorist bombing in 1993. And by the city's fire regulations, the floors were supposed to withstand two hours of fire.

Now the chief's orders came quick: "Tower 1 to all units. Evacuate the building. Evacuate the building."

A police helicopter hovered near the top of the wounded North Tower.

"It looks like it's glowing red," the pilot said. Moments later, he added, "It appears to be buckling."

Not all the firefighters in the tower heard the evacuation order. Some didn't believe it. Others wanted to evacuate as a unit and waited for fire company fellows to gather. Many of the emergency workers climbing the stairs were unaware that the South Tower had collapsed and failed to grasp the urgency of the evacuation order. Some wanted to catch their breath before continuing.

"We'll come down in a few minutes," said one.

When Fire Captain Jay Jonas learned the South Tower had crashed, he said, "It's time to get out of here."

He led a small group of rescuers down a North Tower stairwell. Around the 12th floor, they met a groaning and crying Josephine Harris. Bad feet and a sixty-story descent had brought the office worker to a stop.

"Bring her with us," Jonas said.

They urged her along, but the pace was very, very slow.

At the 4th floor, Josephine quit.

"We're just going to have to drag her," Jonas thought.

Then he felt shaking and the floor rolled like a wave.

The tower pancaked down. With tremendous booms, one floor hit another. Ten stories a second. The banging, screeching, roaring, collapsing floors drove a furious wind ahead of it.

One of Jonas's group was tossed a floor below, another one was thrown three floors down. The others hugged the floor.

A quarter mile—1,350 feet—of glass, metal, plastic, marble, rubber, telephones, copiers, office desks, filing cabinets, ceramic tiles, dry wall, copper pipes, steel sheets, steel beams, and steel rods fell around them. It crushed a neighboring Trade Center office building and demolished the nearby hotel already cleaved in two by the collapsing South Tower.

It was 10:28 AM.

In 102 minutes hijackers had destroyed the World Trade Center, crippled the Pentagon, and doomed four jet liners. 2,973 people were dead, more than the number of Americans killed at Pearl Harbor or on D-Day. It was the largest loss of life on American soil as a result of a hostile attack.

Among the lost were faithful friends Ed Beyea and Abe Zelmanowitz, along with the fireman who didn't desert them, William Burke. Chief Palmer, the first uniformed rescuer to reach the North Tower's 78th floor impact site, perished. Frank De Martini and Pablo Oritz died, too, but not before rescuing scores of others, mostly strangers.

Stanley Praimnath and Brian Clark survived. Trapped elevator passenger Chris Young escaped, too; a surprised fireman discovered him in the North Tower and whisked him to safety. Eighty-nine-year-old Moe Lipson climbed down eighty-eight floors, walked a mile, and then hailed a cab to take him home. The window washer and people in the elevator with him tunneled through drywall and ceramic tiles into a bathroom. They all escaped; the window washer even brought out his bucket and squeegee.

Incredibly, sixteen people survived inside the North Tower, including Captain Jonas's crew. Josephine Harris's pace had been a charm; the building came down all around them but the exact spot where they huddled in the stairwell remained standing. If the group had moved faster or slower, they'd have died in the wreckage. She and the rescuers would later exchange Christmas cards.

Chief Joseph Pfeifer survived, but not his fireman brother. The two last spoke in the North Tower lobby, moments before Lieutenant Kevin Pfeifer led his men up.

Kevin Pfeifer wasn't recovered from the wreckage until February.

Joseph Pfiefer was there.

"Not only did I see him going into the towers, but I also brought him out," said the chief.

Author's Note

The first hours after the events in New York, Washington, D.C., and Pennsylvania on the morning of September 11, 2001 were filled with confusion. Air traffic officials scrambled to check in with airborne planes and eventually grounded them all. Television stations broadcast nothing but images of the attacks. That morning President Bush visited a school in Florida. While reading along with students, an aide told him, "America is under attack." The president was then taken to a secure, undisclosed location.

The entire world felt the impact of that day. Citizens from ninety countries died in the attacks and people from across the globe stood in solidarity with Americans against the threat of terrorism.

Said one Frenchman, "We are all New Yorkers."

In response, the United States turned its might against Afghanistan, the al-Queda safe haven and home to leaders of the September 11 attack. An American invasion ousted the offending Afghan rulers and disrupted al-Qaeda, but failed to capture al-Qaeda leader Osama Bin Laden.

The United States government commissioned an investigation into events of September 11. In 2004, the 9/11 Commission issued a report summarizing the circumstances surrounding the disaster and offering improvements to intelligence gathering, national security, building construction, and emergency response.

The attack on September 11 wrecked buildings, and the cleanup and business disruption of it exacted an economic toll that reached into the hundreds of billions of dollars.

But it is the human cost that is the most sorrowful.

In New York City, 2,749 civilians, emergency workers, airline crew members, and passengers died.

The New York Fire Department lost 343 firefighters. No other emergency agency in history has suffered as many fatalities.

The Port Authority Police lost 37 members. It was the greatest loss of life for any police force in history.

The New York Police Department suffered 32 fatalities, the second largest loss of life of any police force in history.

Both low ranking and senior officers fell. The FDNY Chief of Department and the Port Authority Police Department Superintendent, along with other high-ranking members of their staffs, died.

Of the 2,016 civilians killed in the World Trade Center towers, 658 were employees of one company, Cantor Fitzgerald.

At the Pentagon, 184 people died, including the jetliner crew and passengers.

40 people died in the Shanksville crash.

About 3,000 children lost a parent on that grief-filled day.

Victims of the September 11 attacks could be found throughout New York City and the communities surrounding it. One town, my home of Merrick, New York, lost fifteen people, a number nearly equaling the town's losses to the Vietnam War, and almost as many as killed in World War II. It is to my neighbors that I dedicate this book:

Paul Battaglia   Farrell Lynch

Mark Brisman   Sean Lynch

Herman Broghammer Thomas McHale

Thomas Crotty   Katie McGarry Noack

Ronnie Gies   Brian Sweeney

David Grimner   John Vaccacio

Aram Iskenderian   Frank Vignola Jr.

James Kelly

Bibliography

9/11 Commission. *The 9/11 Commission Report: Final Report of the National Commission on Terrorist Attacks Upon the United States.* New York: W.W. Norton & Co., 2004.

Botte, John. *Aftermath: Unseen 9/11 Photos by a New York City Cop.* New York: Collins Design, 2006.

Dwyer, Jim & Kevin Flynn. *102 Minutes: The Untold Story of the Fight to Survive Inside the Twin Towers.* New York: Time Books, 2005.

Fink, Mitchell & Lois Mathias. *Never Forget: An Oral History of September 11, 2001.* New York: Regan Books, 2002.

Magnum Photographers. *New York September 11.* New York: Powerhouse Books, 2001.

New York City Police Department. *Above Hallowed Ground: A Photographic Record of September 11, 2001.* New York: Penguin, 2002.

New York Times. *A Nation Challenged.* New York: New York Times/Callaway, 2002.

"September 11 by Numbers." *New York* magazine. *http://nymag.com/news/articles/wtc/1year/numbers.htm*

"The Entombed Man's Tale: Jay Jonas." A Day in September: In their Own Voices. *http://archive.recordonline.com/adayinseptember/jonas.htm*

Source Notes

"Something is wrong . . ." 9/11, 6–7.

"Everyone . . . get in the rigs . . ." Fink, 18.

"I heard a roar . . ." Fink, 23.

"We started up . . ." Fink, 219.

"Fire [fighting] systems in the building . . ." 9/11, 291.

"My heart was pumping harder than usual." Fink, 140.

"People were hanging out of the building, gasping for air . . ." Fink, 6.

"There's a second plane!" Dwyer, 131.

"It was a loud roar . . . The building shook . . ." Fink, 146–47.

"The heat inside was so hot, it felt like the sun kissing you." Fink, 153.

"Help! Help! I'm buried! Is anybody there? . . ." Dwyer, 98–99.

"It looked exactly like an avalanche . . ." Fink, 99.

"We saw air conditioning ducts. We saw parts of buildings . . ." Fink, 91.

"I was literally blown out of my shoes." Fink, 82.

"Picture taking . . . flour and sticking it up your nose . . ." Fink, 90–91.

"I thought . . . something was crashing through the lobby . . ." Fink, 20.

"Tower 1 to all units. Evacuate the building . . ." Fink, 20.

"It looks like it's glowing red . . ." Dwyer, 223.

"We'll come down in a few minutes." Dwyer, 227.

"It's time to get out of here." The Entombed Man's Tale.

"Bring her with us . . . We're just going to have to drag her." The Entombed Man's Tale.

"Not only did I see him going into the towers, . . ." Fink, 21.

Library of Congress Cataloging-in-Publication Data

Brown, Don, 1949–
America is under attack : September 11, 2001 : the day the towers fell / Don Brown, — 1st ed.
p.   cm.
ISBN 978-1-59643-694-7
1. September 11 Terrorist Attacks, 2001—Juvenile literature.   2. Terrorism—United States—Juvenile literature.   3. War on Terrorism, 2001–2009—Juvenile literature.   I. Title.

HV6432.7.B767 2011
973.931—dc22

2010045417

First edition 2011
Book design by Andrew Arnold
Printed in May 2011 in China by South China Printing Co. Ltd.,
Dongguan City, Guangdong Province
1 3 5 7 9 8 6 4 2